Naga
9

INDIGENOUS PEOPLES OF THE WORLD

Naga

Grolier Educational Corporation

SHERMAN TURNPIKE, DANBURY, CONNECTICUT 06816

Published by Grolier Educational Corporation 1995
Danbury, Connecticut

Set ISBN: 0-7172-7470-5
Volume ISBN: *Naga* 0-7172-7475-6
Library of Congress Number 94-079533

Manufactured in the United States of America.

Contributors

Jennifer Croft *(Ladakhi)* holds a degree in anthropology from Columbia University and is an editor and free-lance writer.

Anne Johnson *(Inuit, Karenni, Mentawai, Naga)* holds a degree from the University of Wisconsin, Madison. She has done extensive research on myths and folk epics from around the world.

Barbara Miller *(Tuareg)* is a Ph.D. candidate in anthropology at New York University. She specializes in ethnographic filmmaking. She has conducted applied urban research and has been involved with developing curricula for museums and schools.

Eugene Murphy, Ph.D. *(Maya)* is an instructor of anthropology at Columbia University. He has produced an ethnographic documentary on Mayan migration and has written extensively on the peoples of Mexico and China.

Roger Rosen *(Endangered Peoples)* is an editor and publisher. He has published material on the indigenous peoples of the former Soviet Union and has edited numerous articles and papers on the plight of indigenous peoples.

Steven Rubenstein, Ph.D. *(Huaorani)* has been awarded grants in the field of anthropology from the Guggenheim, Fulbright, and MacArthur Foundations and has conducted fieldwork in Brazil, Ecuador, and the United States.

Colleen She *(Miao)* received a master's degree in East Asian studies from Columbia University. She is a free-lance writer and translator.

Jeanne Strazzabosco *(Wayana)* is an instructor in French and Spanish and a free-lance translator and writer whose work regularly addresses the plight of indigenous peoples.

Pegi Vail *(Omo Peoples)* is a Ph.D. candidate in anthropology at New York University. She specializes in visual anthropology and has worked extensively with children's educational programs at museums and schools.

Contents

1. In the Hilltop Village   7

2. The Naga Peoples   11

3. Family and Community   17

4. Customs and Beliefs   27

5. The Colonial Period   39

6. Indian Independence   46

7. A View of the Future   51

Afterword: Neighboring Peoples   57

Facts about the Naga   59

Glossary   60

For Further Reading   62

Index   63

The Naga live in mountain villages nestled along the border between India and Burma.

CHAPTER 1

IN THE HILLTOP VILLAGE

KAITO IS TWELVE YEARS OLD, AND HE HAS A NEW HOME. Along with all the other village boys about his age, he has just been through an initiation ceremony to begin the passage from boyhood to manhood. Kaito looks up shyly at the *morung,* the huge building where he and the other initiates will live from today until they marry. "Surely it will be many years before I take a wife," he thinks. "I hope I like it in the *morung!*"

The building is made of wood and is decorated with huge carvings celebrating a bird called the hornbill. Everybody knows that the hornbill is the symbol of a brave warrior, but today that thought is a little frightening to Kaito. As an initiate in the *morung,* his duty will be to learn the arts of the warrior. If he is successful and bright, he may also be trained as a community leader in the years to come. It is overwhelming, thinking of all the things a person has to learn. He whispers a prayer to a carving of an oxlike animal called a mithan. It is appropriate for Kaito to ask a mithan for kindness. They are such nice beasts that they inspire folksongs about their gentle nature.

When they are about twelve years old, Naga boys such as this Zemi Naga boy take part in an initiation ceremony.

Kaito's eyes travel down the rugged hillside. He can see his father's lands, newly cleared for sowing. What a lot of work it was to chop down all those trees. Kaito remembers the ache in his arms the next day, and the smell of the smoke when the felled trees were burned. It had looked as if the whole world was on fire. Sure, he had complained about the work then; all the children in his work group liked to grumble sometimes. But now these memories make Kaito sad. No longer will he cut branches alongside his sister, or meet children from other clans during harvest. Now he will not work his own family's field, but will labor only for the *morung*. He must think of them as his new family, as his mother has told him.

How proud she was when he was initiated. Kaito fingers the bright woven belt that his mother made as a gift for him. She told him that he was brave, and Kaito feels a lump in his throat as he pictures her pounding rice into flour early in the morning in front of the family hut. He knows that his mother is also brave. Once Kaito's father took him down a path leading to an old family plot of land. The land had been resting for many years because its soil had grown weak. But among the weeds in the path they found a stone set up on end. "This is your stone, my son," said his father. "Your mother was so strong and healthy when she carried you in her belly that she went to work every day. You were born in this field while she was sowing the new crop. We set up this stone to mark your birth, since it brought a great blessing on the field."

Kaito smiles now to think of his father's words. Turning to the *morung,* he lifts his chin and throws his shoulders back. He's going to be a great leader, he thinks. No longer afraid of his future, Kaito steps bravely into the beautiful doorway and joins the other boys as they gather for their lessons. "I am lucky," the young warrior thinks. "At birth my first monument was raised in my honor. Some people must wait until they are grown before they have stones raised for them. Something must be done to return the respect that was shown to me at my birth. I shall be a good student, a brave fighter, and a respected leader. If I become rich, I'll share my wealth with the whole village by holding many huge, elegant feasts. Even the poorest people will eat meat and drink rice beer until they are stuffed and happy."▲

The Naga fight for independence was actually sparked by the British colonial government, which introduced the idea that the Naga were one people. Today, Indian army camps in Naga villages are evidence of the tension between the Naga and the government.

CHAPTER 2

THE NAGA PEOPLES

THE NORTHEAST OF INDIA ADJOINS THE COUNTRY OF BURMA (or Myanmar, as it has been renamed) in a hilly borderland. The steep, fertile hillsides have been cut deep with terraces used for farmland. On both sides of the border, along the crests of the hills, live many groups of people, all of whom are called Naga.

It takes some investigation to learn why the many Naga groups are branches of one fundamental group. It is not even agreed how many branches there are; some say thirteen, some say thirty. The linguistic roots are the same for all. They speak languages of the Tibeto-Burman family; however, the variations are so great that sometimes neighboring villages cannot understand each other.

In fact, it has been only in the last few generations that the Naga have thought of themselves as a unified people. Before that each of the hundreds of Naga villages lived strictly to itself, with occasional trade, warfare, or intermarriage with other hill villages. It was the British colonial government that imposed the idea that all the Naga villages were a single entity. That idea planted the seed that grew into the unified federation of Naga nations, an essential element of the current political struggle in northeast India. The diverse cultures have recognized their common origins and have joined together to fight for their independence and ethnic identity.

The Naga number more than one million. About half a million of them live in the Indian state of Nagaland. The rest dwell in the hills of western Myanmar and the Indian states of Assam, Manipur, and Arunachal Pradesh. The peoples migrated to their hilltop homes over the course of hundreds of years. It is generally thought that most of them came from the east (that is, through Myanmar) about 2,000 years ago. They have prehistoric roots in common with many peoples throughout the world, including Polynesians, Chinese, Indonesians, and even some Native Americans.

Although the Naga groups are related to one another, each has its own myth about how it came to its current homeland. The Sangtam Naga believe that their ancestors traveled from the southeast. The Konyak, the largest Naga group, have more than one belief, some subgroups claiming roots in the south and some in the northeast. A tradition of the Ao Naga group holds that their ancestors sprang from six sacred stones in the southeast.

One of the most important factors that bind the Naga groups together is that they all live on hilltops. All have similar agricultural and building practices suited to their environment.

NAGALAND

CHINA

INDIA

Nagaland

BURMA
(Myanmar)

ASSAM

NORTH CACHAR
HILLS DISTRICT

Konyak

Phom

Ao

Chang

Lhota

Sema

Kalyo-Kengyu

NAGA HILLS DISTRICT

BURMA
(Myanmar)

W. Rengma

UNADMINISTERED
AREA

Angami

Sangtam

Kabui

MANIPUR

Most groups share a story explaining how the hills were formed: When the world was being made, a crow was given the duty of flattening out the land. He did well as he made the plains, but he got a bellyache and quit before he got to the Naga hills. No one ever did get around to leveling off that area.

Because the crow failed to flatten the hills, the Naga have had to make special adaptations. Ordinary farming techniques are not effective on sloping, forested land. The first form of agriculture taken up by the Naga was known as *jhum* or "slash-and-burn." The flattest possible areas were chosen first. Work groups chopped down all the trees on the plot, using long blades called *dhou*. Then the felled trees and undergrowth were

Rice, millet, and maize are among the crops raised by Naga farmers. Crops
are cultivated by the slash-and-burn method and by terracing.

cleared away by setting fire to the field. The *jhumed* land was used to grow dry rice, millet, taro, maize, ginger, chillies, and cotton.

After two years of cultivation, the land would be allowed to rest for ten years before another crop was planted. During the fallow period, more and more plots of land were cleared and cultivated. There has been some concern that slash-and-burn cultivation is harmful to the environment. Some Naga, therefore, especially the Angami, have adopted a system called terracing, with which it is possible to farm on the steepest hillside, where the soil has never been used before. Level areas are dug into the sides of hills, like giant steps. The most important crop grown on terrace plots is wet rice; that is, rice grown in man-made swamps or paddies.

The Naga have always survived chiefly as farmers. Harvesting any crop by hand is heavy work. It is no wonder that several Naga groups share a story about how, long ago, people had only to call the rice and it would come on its own, flying to the village from the fields!

The crops grown by farmers are the main food sources for the Naga. They also keep domestic animals such as fowl, pigs, and the huge mithan, a cross-breed of ox and bison. Livestock is mostly eaten on feast days, when it has been sacrificed in a ritual. Game is also obtained by hunting. Although much of the area wildlife is endangered today, 19th-century reports tell of the great bounty of animals that "swarmed" the Naga country: elephant, monkey, leopard, tiger, wild buffalo, rhinoceros, deer, wild boar, civet (a wild cat), bear, porcupine, pheasant, partridge, and peacock.

The Naga have applied their ingenuity to the problem of fishing. They devised traps that fish could swim into but not escape. In another technique known as "poisoning," the sap of the creeper plant is put into an area of water. It creates a chemical reaction that removes the oxygen from the water, causing the fish to float to the top. The hills are home to the Naga, and they have adapted their culture so that they can survive and prosper. Generations of intervention by the British colonial government and the Indian independent government have threatened their sense of identity. The hill peoples themselves, along with all who are concerned about human rights throughout the world, are now faced with the question: Who are the Naga?▲

CHAPTER 3

FAMILY AND COMMUNITY

AT THE HEART OF "NAGA" IS THE VILLAGE. THE BRITISH colonizers found hundreds of Naga villages and categorized them into "tribes," based on language and cultural similarities. However, the Naga considered each village as a separate, self-governing unit. The villages were built on hilltops where they could be easily defended. With plenty of fertile land and a good water supply, each was self-sufficient. Wide valleys separated the hills, so it was difficult for villages to keep in contact with each other.

The differences among villages are remarkable; it is sometimes hard to see what they have in common. The easiest way to understand the similarities is to view their systems as falling between two extremes: egalitarian and hierarchic.

The Angami are the most egalitarian of all the Naga groups. Although each Angami village is different from any other, they all share the trait of having no chief and no clan ranking system. A Naga village with an egalitarian system of government is called *thenkoh*. An official village leader, the *tevo*, has only ritual significance; the *tevo* is believed to be a direct descendant of the village founder. Decisions in a *thenkoh* village are made by a group of community elders.

At the other end of the spectrum are the Konyak with the hierarchic system, *thendu*. Their villages are governed by powerful chiefs called *angs*, who are both political and religious rulers. The *ang* has as much power as a king, and his reign is often threatened by jealous persons who want to overthrow him.

Between the Angami and the Konyak fall the other Naga villages. Their cultural differences largely reflect the extent to which their society is *thenkoh* or *thendu*.

Each village is divided into two or more wards, or *khels*. People are grouped into *khels* partly depending on clan, although the system differs among the villages. Within the *khels*, individual families set up households.

The family's domestic animals live outside of the hut. Inside the hut, the main room is the living and sleeping quarters. Baskets of dried foods are hung from the ceiling, and tools such as spears and the *dhou* blade are stored in the corners. A small room at the front is used for pounding rice. This part of the house is raised up on wooden stilts to protect it from floods. The back porch is a place for women to weave in the daytime and for the family to relax after a hard day's work. Men and women tell each other the day's news as the sun sets, while their children play and delight in the whirring of carved wooden tops.

An individual's identity is based on his or her family, clan, *khel*, and village. This young woman is a member of the Zemi Naga.

An Angami Naga woman uses the back porch of her home for weaving.

The Morung

When children reach the age of about twelve, their lives change as they prepare to become adults. Boys are sent to live in the *morung*. This large wooden building is more than just a boarding school. Naga society is classified by the *morung* to which people belong. In the more egalitarian villages, such as those of the Ao Naga, the *morung* is the largest building in the village. Among the more hierarchical Naga, the *ang*'s house is larger than the *morung*. The *morung* serves as social and ritual center for all its members and their families. A person remains attached to his *morung* for life. Some areas have an equivalent building for girls.

The original purpose of the *morung* was to train young men to be warriors. The initiation ceremony for boys passing into puberty was full of actions symbolizing a raid on an enemy village. Sometimes a tree was chosen to represent the enemy, and the initiates had to throw spears hard enough to stick into its trunk. In other villages, the boys were led into enemy territory, although they did not engage in fighting until they were trained.

Protecting the village and raiding neighbors were means of survival for all the Naga peoples. Much of the economy was based on making enemies or allies out of other villages. The successful work of a brave young warrior not only kept his village safe, but also brought new wealth to his people. For this reason, the *morung* symbolized the prosperity of the village. The initiates lived in the *morung* from about age twelve until their marriage a few years later. They were taught by elders about the oral history of the people and their role as adults in society.

Marriage

All the Naga are exogamous, meaning that they must marry outside of their societal group. For some villages that group is the clan, for some the *khel*, and for some it is the *morung*. The only exception to this rule is the *ang* of the Konyak. His power is partly based upon ancestry, so he may marry within his own clan to keep the royal bloodline pure.

Although young people now can choose their own spouse, at one time marriages were encouraged that would form a useful

Among the Konyak Naga, the *ang* is a very powerful figure.

alliance with another *morung* or village. Once an engagement has been accepted by the village leaders, tokens of respect such as spearheads and rice beer are exchanged between the two groups to solidify the agreement.

Marriage practices also vary greatly among the Naga groups. Among the Sema and the Konyak, strictly hierarchical societies, rules are strict. The groom is required to pay a high bridewealth to his father-in-law. This bridewealth is sometimes paid in cash today, but traditionally it was a long sequence of exchange of goods that could last for generations. The groom might also be required to work on his father-in-law's fields for a certain length of time as part of the bridewealth.

Work

Once a married couple have set up a household, and the man has been released from working for his father-in-law, they may begin to keep their own land. In some of the *thenkoh* (egalitarian) villages, individual families can own land, but the *thendu* groups tend to keep land by *khel* or clan.

In a farming society, there is much hard work to be done. Even children are expected to help, and at a young age they are organized into work groups. These groups often cross *khel*, clan, and *morung* lines and provide a way for children to meet each other. Even an *ang*'s child is expected to work alongside the other children.

Next to cultivating the land, trading has been the second most important source of income for the Naga. Today the trading center is Wakching village in the Konyak area. The Naga have a long history of trading with each other and with the plains people. According to 13th-century records of the hill peoples, they traded salt, cotton, chillies, ginger, ivory, and palm leaf mats to the people of the plains. In return they received dried fish, cowrie shells, brass, wire, cattle, and—later—gunpowder. Both men and women worked as traders.

Social Status

To the Naga, land represents wealth. Owners of large lands can produce abundant crops, and the village depends on them to supplement the general food supply. This is done by a distinctive Naga tradition called the Feast of Merit.

The Feasts of Merit redistribute the wealth of the community, because everyone in the village is invited to participate in the ceremonies and partake of the bounty. A second purpose is to raise the social status of the person who can afford such extravagance. With each feast the person climbs another rung on the village social ladder. In other words, the more a person shares his or her wealth with the community, the more he or she is respected.

There is a series of Feasts of Merit, each level requiring a greater expenditure than the last. Besides supplying huge quantities of rice beer, the host is expected to provide several mithan for sacrifice (the people then eat the meat) and raise monuments of stone and wood. With each level of feast that a person reaches, he is allowed to wear new marks of importance. Most of the Naga groups have special ornaments

One's position on the Naga social ladder is determined in large part on the basis of who owns the most land.

In the city of Kohima, Angami Naga students take part in a traditional festival celebrating their culture.

that indicate social status: round brass badges worn by feast hosts, cotton ear pads worn by Konyak rulers, or weaving designs designating particular clans.

Feasts of Merit are most popular among the *thenkoh* Naga villages, representing an opportunity for individuals to gain importance in the community. Anyone who gains enough wealth can throw a feast. In the more hierarchic villages, the ruling class is not comfortable with the idea of lower-class persons getting ahead in society, even if only symbolically.▲

CHAPTER 4

CUSTOMS AND BELIEFS

ONCE UPON A TIME, A MAN WAS SQUATTING DOWN TO SHARPEN *his* dhou *blade when along came a crayfish and pinched him on the behind. The man was so startled that he jerked the* dhou *forward and cut off the tops of some bamboo shoots. The flying bamboo chips struck a wildfowl, and the frightened bird accidentally clawed a red ant. Wounded, the angry ant stung a passing wild boar. "Ow!" said the boar and ran head-first into a banana tree. The bat sleeping in the tree was scared out of its mind and flew right into an elephant's ear. The elephant jumped out of its reveries and trampled an old widow's hut.*

The widow was very upset and demanded an explanation. "But the bat started it when it flew into my ear," protested the elephant. The widow then went to the bat, who blamed the wild boar, and so on down the line, until the dhou *sharpener blamed the crayfish for nipping his behind. All the animals cornered the crayfish. "Why did you pinch the* dhou *sharpener?" they demanded. But the crayfish just shrugged, scratched its head with its big claw, and jumped into a deep pond, never to be seen again.*

Among the Naga, oral history is both a means of entertainment and a way of passing on information. These young Angami men gather to swap stories at a festival.

In a culture where oral history is the main teaching tool, each story contains a lesson about society. The Naga story of the *dhou* sharpener contains examples of some native animals and their typical behavior when frightened. It also shows how everything a person does in a village affects everyone else, and the importance of taking responsibility for your own actions.

Some stories explain the way things are. For example, the Ao Naga traditionally made fire with a split stick, a stone, and a bamboo thong, an instrument called a firestick. They have a myth telling how this custom started: Fire and water have always been enemies. Once fire was running from water and hid in some bamboo. A monkey, who was cold, saw fire hide and fashioned a firestick out of a branch, a stone, and the bamboo until the fire was forced out. A human saw the monkey do this and stole the firestick. This is why people use firesticks today, but monkeys need fur to keep warm.

Spirits and Souls

Most Naga villages were traditionally animist societies. They believed that spirits existed within everything. In this belief system, the supernatural was often used to explain the ways of the world. Prayers were used to please the spirits so that they would give good fortune to the community and ward off illness and disaster:

> Today we offer a mithan to you.
> May there be no more rain today.
> May all be well.
> May all of our men and women prosper.
> Give us good crops.   (Sangtam prayer)

The Naga groups generally believe in three types of spirits: a high god who created the world, a sky spirit, and earthly spirits. The *thendu* Konyak, with their ruling-class system, put great emphasis on their highest god, Gawang, who is all-powerful and remote. In their religious capacity, the village *angs* are sacred chiefs of Gawang. On the other hand, the *thenkoh* Angami have a female creator spirit, Kepenopfu. She is assisted by the *terhomia,* earth spirits who constantly affect everyday life: the household, hunting, fertility, and bad luck. When the Angami make sacrifices, it is usually to the *terhomia.*

The Ao Naga, of which this woman is a member, have a myth explaining why they use firesticks to make fire. According to the myth, humans stole them from monkeys.

A common thread among all the Naga groups is a relationship between humans and leopards and tigers. It is possible for a person's soul to be possessed by a wildcat. The human soul lives in the cat's body but returns to the human during dreams to inform him or her of where it has been. Sema and Konyak women are most prone to leopard and tiger possession. It may be that in these male-dominated hierarchical societies this is the only way a woman can gain any power or freedom of expression.

Most Naga groups believe that each person has at least two kinds of soul. One of these is fixed in the person during his lifetime. When the person dies, this soul goes to the land of the dead. The other soul is looser and is constantly in danger of being attacked by angry spirits. That is what has happened if a person becomes sick. For the person to be cured, a sacrifice must be made to the angry spirit so that it will release the person's soul.

Such a sacrifice must be performed by a ritual specialist trained in the arts of contact with the spirit world. The Lhota Naga have two varieties of specialist, called *ratsen* (shaman) and *puthi* (priest). The *ratsen* can speak with the spirit world in his dreams. If a person is sick, the *ratsen* asks a spirit for guidance in the cure. The *puthi* is almost like a political representative among the spirits. This hereditary position involves a life of severe restrictions. The entire village is embodied in the *puthi*, and anything that the priest does wrong has bad effects on his whole society.

Festivals and Genna

The idea of restrictions, or *genna*, is central to all Naga religion. Festival periods are always marked with sacrifices, feasts, dancing, and long periods of restricted behavior. Breaking these taboos is thought to anger the spirits and bring bad luck. The two most important *genna* are a taboo on agricultural work for a certain period, and restrictions on entering and leaving the boundaries of a village.

The Tulani festival of the Sema is typical of the customs and purposes of a Naga ritual period. Tulani is celebrated in July and is designed to please the gods of the harvest. The village priest, or *awou,* fixes the proper day for the festival to begin.

Each crop has its own guardian spirit, and each one must be honored. Tulani used to last for weeks, but now it has been reduced to seven days. On the first day millet wine is made. The *genna* against leaving the village begins and lasts throughout the festival. Rice wine is brewed by men of high status on the second day. On the third day each family stays at home and has a meal of pork, which they offer to a god. The god Litsaba, protector of crops, is celebrated on the fourth day. Families go from house to house, visiting and sharing feasts and prayers. The fifth day finds the men and boys of the village joining forces to spruce up the area, clearing paths, washing buildings, cleaning out wells. In the evening they celebrate their hard work with sports and war dances. The women have the sixth day for their rituals and

Young people may take part in dancing during Naga festivals, as demonstrated by these Zemi Naga youths at a full-moon celebration.

dance. On the final day of Tulani, it is taboo to enter the fields. To see the moon on that night is thought to assure a good crop.

Festivals such as Tulani focus on village unity and independence from the outside world. They also have the practical purpose of keeping the village in good condition and giving the people a rest from their hard work. Most Naga villages have a central area for ritual sacrifices and community meetings. For the Zemi, a tilted block of stone, *hazoa*, is the ritual center. The Angami have a sacred point for each *khel*, in the form of a wooden gate that is erected with great ceremony. The Lhota build their village around a sacred tree. If this tree is damaged, a series of rituals must be held to renew the purity of the village.

Woodcarving and Other Crafts

For many Naga groups, the *morung* serves as the communal and ritual center. The large building, sometimes as much as 50 feet long, is decorated with symbols of the village's strength and unity. Hornbills, mithans, tigers, and human skulls are carved out of wood by skilled craftsmen to make the *morung* even more impressive. In front of the *morung* is a huge drum made of a tree trunk. The tree for the "log gong" is chosen by the village priest for its perfection. Among the Ao Naga villages a log gong can be as long as 35 feet. The middle is hollowed out, but the two ends are left intact, and on these is carved the likeness of the head and tail of a mithan. When struck with a mallet, this drum makes a deep

Some crafts may be restricted during festival periods in order to avoid bad luck and the anger of the spirits.

sound that matches its size and can be heard throughout the hills. Originally the log gong was used as a war cry, but now it is struck to call people to festivals and to warn of emergency situations.

The Phom Naga are particularly skilled woodcarvers, whereas other Naga groups have other craft specialties. Certain men in Ao and Rengma villages are known for the designs they paint on cloth to show the social status of the wearer. The Sema are famed for their weaving, and the Konyak for their intricate tattoo arts.

Often the *gennas* or taboos that accompany a festival period apply to crafts. The creative forces of both farming and the

35

The *morung* a boy will enter is often chosen when he is still a baby. This mother and her children belong to an isolated Naga group in Burma.

arts must be kept under tight control. The Rengma may not make pottery after sowing millet. Once the new crop of rice has sprouted, the Konyak are forbidden to carve wood and the Rengma must not work with metal.

Growing Up Naga

All these customs and beliefs affect a Naga from infancy. A newborn child is surrounded by ritual. In the Zemi villages one of the first things to be done when a baby is born is to choose its *morung*. This is done by a symbolic contest. Old men and women from various *morungs* compete to be the first to tie a thread around the child's tiny wrist. Whichever *morung* is represented by the winner can claim the child as an initiate when he comes of age. A baby receives its name from the father's clan or an adjective that describes some good quality such as bravery or beauty. On the second day after birth, a child's ear is pierced and a lock of its hair cut off by the father to welcome it into the clan.

Until they reach puberty, children learn by watching and listening to their parents. They are taught about the world by means of stories. They learn to imitate the parent of the same sex, so that the gender roles of the community are passed on.

Once boys—and sometimes girls—have gone into the *morung*, their education is structured much as in a high school. Academic subjects, physical education, recreation, crafts, and music are all part of the curriculum. In some Naga communities where Western-style schools have a stronghold, the *morung* has lost most of its original purpose.

Today many of the traditional Naga customs are still practiced. However, outside interference has interrupted the self-sufficiency of the villages. In fact, this interference has led to a change in the Nagas' fundamental view of themselves.▲

CHAPTER 5

THE COLONIAL PERIOD

WHEN EUROPEANS FIRST CAME IN CONTACT WITH THE NAGA groups in the early 1800s, they were puzzled. These villages seemed to be hundreds of separate republics, with different languages, arts, and political systems. They warred and made alliances with each other as if they were separate peoples. Yet they were somehow all alike.

To the British, who were in the process of colonizing India and Burma in the 1820s, the Naga were categorized as one people because they lived on the border between the two countries. Throughout the period of British contact with the Naga over the next 120 years, this was an important issue.

The Naga learned this fact early. In 1824 Britain took over Burma in a long, bloody struggle. The Naga were caught in the middle, and their hills became battlegrounds and outposts for British troops. Much property was destroyed or seized, whole villages were burned, and Naga lives were lost in this imperialist war that did not even involve the Naga.

By the 1840s the British were firmly entrenched as the colonial government in India and Burma. They were strenuously affecting the lives of many of their new "subject" peoples, forcing changes in religion, ritual practices, and education, and seizing farmland for use by European settlers. At first, the Naga were not touched by such policies. The British decided that it was not worth the expense to enforce a new lifestyle among them. The hilly Naga homeland protected them from intervention. The colonizers could see no profit to be gained from rugged terrain that was so difficult to farm. They were interested in flat lands on which to grow crops like coffee and tea, which sold at high prices in export. The only time the British paid much attention to the Naga was when violent raids were staged against British villages in the plains below the Naga hills.

The policy of nonintervention could not last forever. Always in need of more money to support the colony, the British expanded their interests into Naga territory to seize land for growing tea. In 1866, the Naga Hills District was established, and the Naga fought hard to defend their land from invasion. The villagers made enough trouble that the British wrote a territory regulation that was supposed to protect most of Naga territory. Even into the late 20th century, this Inner Line Regulation continues to be updated periodically, with each revision seizing more land from the Naga.

In spite of the Inner Line Regulation, the British would not leave the northeast frontier in peace. The year 1879 was historic as the first time that several Naga villages joined

In the 1800s, the Naga put up a strong fight against British invasion. The solidarity displayed then is still evident in political battles today.

forces to fight the British. In this War of Naga Independence, thirteen Angami villages and the capital city of Kohima united in protest against the British presence on their land.

The result of this uprising was a change in British policy. The colonizers hired Naga people to work in their own villages to keep law and order on behalf of the British. Called *gaonburas*, these Naga deputies were supposed to represent the interests of both the government and their own ethnic group. Clearly, this policy had a self-contained conflict of interests. During the period of the *gaonburas*, the Naga were beginning to explore a new source of power: unity.

It is generally agreed that World War I brought about the first unification of all the Naga peoples. Britain was desperate for soldiers and in 1916-17 recruited 4,000 Naga men. For the first time, the many Naga groups reached out to each other, trying to understand the cruelty and senseless loss of life brought by this war. The British had considered the Naga barbaric because of their intervillage warfare, but a Naga village rarely lost more than one or two people per year in raids. Here were the supposedly "civilized" races slaughtering each other by the thousands and forcing the Naga to take part.

The Naga could not forget their sons who died in World War I, and they have never since lost their sense of unity. The end of the war left these peoples searching for their common identity. They felt a need to establish a new cultural definition of the word Naga.

The Effects of Colonialism

To make the Naga villages "manageable," the British classified the settlements into about thirteen "tribes," including such designations as Angami, Konyak, Sema, Zemi, Rengma, Lhota, and Sangtam. Anthropologists and missionaries were responsible for applying these names in the late 19th century, and over the years the Naga became accustomed to referring to themselves in this way.

The basic reason for inventing Naga tribes was to facilitate taxation; it grouped these hundreds of separate villages into administrative units. Taxation had a profound effect on Naga

Taxation by the British was particularly difficult for egalitarian groups like the Angami Naga, who here take part in a traditional ceremony.

culture. The so-called "house tax" was charged to every Naga family. It was the first time that most Naga had needed money. No longer could a village be self-sufficient. Young men and women were forced to leave their villages to take jobs as laborers on railway and road-building projects, in coal mines, and on tea plantations. Socially, taxation was most difficult for egalitarian societies such as the Angami. Never before had members of a *thenkoh* village felt the direct control of a central authority.

Some writers believe that the introduction of Christianity was the most important change that came to the Naga during the colonial period. The American Baptist Mission did the most work in the area. They were able to convert the Naga because they presented the new religion in a way that did not seem to conflict with Naga traditional beliefs. It has been argued that Christianity greatly damaged Naga culture, but the missionaries were a strong influence in forming the people's self-image. Intervillage churches brought members of Naga groups together for the first time, making them realize their similar situations and struggles.▲

Because of the challenges they have faced over many years, the Naga have a strong self-image and sense of unity.

CHAPTER 6

INDIAN INDEPENDENCE

BY THE LATE 1920S IT WAS OBVIOUS THAT INDIA WOULD soon gain independence from Great Britain. The Naga Club and the Naga National Council (NNC) were formed for the purpose of planning an independent Naga nation. They did not want to be part of India, because they did not think of themselves as Indian. Unfortunately, however, when independence came to India in 1947, the new government thought of the Naga territory as a valuable asset. The Naga petition to be left out of the Indian Union was ignored, and the Naga Hills area was placed under the control of the state of Assam. As a result, the Naga became a political minority.

The NNC was by this time divided about the problem. One faction had broken off from the original cause of independence and was now interested in setting up a system of self-rule for the Naga within the Indian Union. They reasoned that the relatively small Naga population could never hope to overcome the Indian government, but could perhaps benefit from India's assistance or protection. The other main faction of the NNC

The Naga formed a strong rebel movement to resist Indian control of the Naga region.

was vehemently in favor of an utterly independent Naga nation. It was this group that attracted the attention of a remarkable Angami man named A. Zapho Phizo.

Phizo was an outspoken supporter of self-determination for the Naga, an active member of the radical faction of the NNC in the 1940s. Frustrated by its internal struggles, he left that group to form the People's Independent League (PIL), dedicated to the cause of all-Naga independence. The PIL wanted a self-ruled Nagaland that included not only the Naga Hills, but also Tuensang and the neighboring Naga areas in Assam, Manipur, and Burma. Phizo's vision and energy had a profound effect on the Naga people, and the Indian government found him threatening. After he had rallied public enthusiasm by forming the Naga Youth Movement and the Naga Women's Society, the government jailed him briefly in 1949 for plotting against the Indian Union.

Naga solidarity was possibly Phizo's major achievement. As president of the NNC in 1951, he actually conducted a survey of all the Naga, which proved two main points: (1) that the great majority wanted independence from India, and (2) that the NNC did not represent just a few powerful Naga personages. Although the Naga in Burma were unable to respond to the survey because of government interference, the evidence was overwhelming that India's Naga people supported the fight for freedom.

Growing Protest

Now the sense of a unified Naga federation was stronger than ever, and serious protests against India were taking place. By 1953 civil disobedience and boycotts against government meetings and elections were so prevalent that the government of Assam sent in troops to control this "disturbed area." The newsletter of the NNC was banned, as if that would quell the fervor for independence. Instead, boycotts reached an unprecedented level. Naga all over the area quit civil service jobs and walked out of government meetings. Even menial laborers refused to work.

Entirely illegally, the Naga formed their own government in 1956. The Naga Federal Government wrote a constitution that stated very clearly what it wanted: that each Naga village should be a republic in its own right; that each family or tribe that owned land should have control over its land. There were also provisions for freedom of expression and of religion, and even a clause guaranteeing equal pay for men and women.

As expected, the Indian government saw this rival government as a dangerous conspiracy. For months a bloody war was waged between the strong Indian forces and the Naga troops, who numbered only 500 and were not fully trained. Many lives were lost, and as villages were burned and fields destroyed the inhabitants of the hills sometimes had to flee into the jungle for safety.

In 1957 a Naga Peoples Convention was convened in hopes of finding some solution other than bloodshed. The participants were ready to work within the Union of India, since they did not think total independence was worth a fight to the death. The result of the convention was the formation of the Indian state of Nagaland. Unlike Phizo's vision of a state that would include all Naga areas, Nagaland covers only the Naga Hills and the Tuensang area, or about half of the Naga population.

Meanwhile the extreme Naga nationalists continued the war for freedom. Over the years the nationalists split and took sides against each other, a situation that the Indian government often used to its own advantage. Bloodshed and guerrilla fighting became so intense that in 1975 the state of Nagaland was put under direct control of the President of India.

Under the President's eye, the underground rebel movement had no choice but to reach some sort of agreement with India. Representatives of the rebel movement signed the

Oil is one of the coveted natural resources found in the Naga region.

Shillong Accord in that year, agreeing to turn in their arms, accept the Indian constitution, and agree to a long period of negotiation. The Naga rebel movement split in 1980, some rebels holding that the Shillong Accord was surrender, which they were not ready to accept. An extremist group called the National Socialist Council of Nagaland was formed. This council has a large following and a trained army of over 4,000 troops.▲

CHAPTER 7

A VIEW OF THE FUTURE

IN THE 1990S THE STRUGGLE FOR NAGA INDEPENDENCE continues, both in India and in Burma. Nationalist Naga do not recognize as legitimate any official government borders. The current Indian state of Nagaland excludes the Naga of Assam, Arunachal Pradesh, Manipur, and Burma. In the nationalist point of view, all Naga are one. They prefer to think of each Naga group as a small nation, and they are fighting for a united federation of Naga nations.

Even within Nagaland, the Naga feel that they are being exploited by the Indian government. The area has great potential for wealth because of its natural resources. The Naga want to exploit these resources themselves, and they complain that the Indian government is reaping all the benefit. The hills have oil resources, but India has already contracted with oil companies to prospect there. The forest has been greatly depleted in the last few decades, especially by the Indian armies, who appropriated Naga timber for fires and building. Most tantalizing are the confidential reports about possible mineral wealth in the hills. Rumors of gold and uranium have the Naga worried that their land will become the site of mines as the government exploits their resources. The loss of this potential for income is damaging to the prospects of a free Naga Federation in the future. The Naga also fear that India will exploit these resources only with an eye for profit, without concern for the effects on the environment.

Population Problems

Another major concern for the Naga is the change in population in former Naga areas. The Indian government has begun industrializing the area, establishing paper mills and sugar factories, then selling them to corporations. The result is that hundreds of thousands of plains people have moved into Naga towns. It is not the introduction of new people, but the scale of population change that is alarming. For example, towns such as Tuli and Dimapur, once with populations of several thousand, have each been inundated with 20,000 plains people since their factories opened. Some Naga accuse the Indian government of purposely trying to make the Naga a minority in their own hills to reduce their power. There are also less direct results of the population changes. For example, each year Nagaland is granted a certain number of entrants into Indian universities. In recent years some plains people have been applying for and receiving those coveted Naga places, arguing that they live in Nagaland and are therefore Naga. Each time this happens, one more Naga

Naga nationalism has become a sophisticated political campaign. The assassination of several Naga independence leaders sparked this demonstration in Kohima.

student fails to go to the university.

Many Naga, both men and women, are well educated, as is obvious from the sophisticated political battles they have waged in this century. Naga nationalists are quite westernized in many senses, from wearing Western clothes to being familiar with modern warfare techniques. A new unofficial language has arisen. Nicknamed Nagamese, it is a combination of Assamese, Bengali, and Hindi. Among a people with at least thirty dialects, it is useful to have a language that allows communication not only among villages, but also with the plains people.

At the same time, the hilltop villagers still speak their original dialects of Tibeto-Burman. While the leaders of their federation are struggling to put on a powerful unified front, each Naga village is encouraged to keep to its traditional, isolated ways. As young people receive Western education, they question their parents' customs. Islam and Hinduism are spreading to the Naga cities with the plains people who come to work there. Among the Naga themselves, between 80 and 95 percent have converted to Christianity.

The conflict between Christianity and Naga animism is symbolic of the many conflicts faced by the Naga today. A very few pay no attention to Christianity. A larger number have become Christian in the European sense and have disowned traditional practices that they consider "unchristian." The great majority of Naga Christians are working to form a unique blend of animism and Christianity. One Naga recently wrote that his Angami upbringing allowed him to experience Christianity in a unique way. The Angami *terhomia*, or earthly spirits, come to him in dreams and help him to communicate with the Christian God.

It is just this sort of adjustment and personal exploration that will help the Naga through their period of struggle. There is no easy answer to their conflicts. Some Naga believe that it is worth giving their lives to free their people. Others, just as proud to be Naga, think it better to leave things as they are and bring peace to their land. During this struggle, they must continue to seek their true identity. The word Naga stands both for many peoples and for one people.▲

Traditional customs continue to encourage cultural unity within communities.
Young Angami Naga men and women make a spirit offering in the *morung*.

Political and environmental changes happening today will shape the fate of future Naga generations.

NEIGHBORING PEOPLES

BEFORE THE BRITISH CAME TO INDIA, THE MOST IMPORTANT neighbors of the Naga were the **Ahom**. The Ahom inhabited the plains region around the Brahmaputra River, which runs north of Nagaland from east to west. In 1228 this powerful group had taken control of the plains regions and was trying to subjugate the Naga hill peoples as well. The Naga-Ahom relationship continued for 600 years and is partly documented in records kept at the royal court of Ahom. Throughout this period, power switched from one party to the other as alliances were formed and broken. The Ahom called all the hill peoples Naga in general, and it is now impossible to say to which villages they were referring.

The **Mising** people of Assam had the role of middlemen in trade between Ahom and Naga. They live today on the flood-prone banks of the Brahmaputra River. Rather than being threatened by the floods, the Mising have learned that the swollen waters bring rich nutrients to their soil. The distinctive floral patterns of their weaving and their gold and coral jewelry are typical of the Mising love of beauty. With the Naga they share an important cultural trait: Until recently, Mising villages were dominated by a large *morung* where the boys were trained for manhood.

The largest of the plains groups is the **Boro-Kachari**, an ancient people who came to northern India from China through Tibet. "Boro" refers to the Tibetan language. The Boro-Kachari were rulers of Assam, rivaling even the powerful Ahom kingdom. These people still live in the districts of Goalpara, Kamurp, and Darrang, practicing their traditional culture mixed with Hinduism. The legacy of the Boro-Kachari comes mostly from their brilliant inventiveness. Of the technologies that they introduced to northern India, the most important is the silk culture. Because of Boro-Kachari influence, many other peoples of Assam supplement their agricultural income by raising silkworms and weaving silk.

In Manipur, to the south, the **Meitei** were the strongest people, even during the early period of British occupation. In fact, some historians believe that the British persuaded the Meitei king to help them take control of the Naga peoples in the area. The Tangkhul Naga, in the eastern hills of Manipur, were the only hill people who could challenge the Meitei.

Because of the changing definition of the word Naga, it is a matter of debate which peoples in Manipur are Naga. For example, the **Maring** are a large group living at the edge of the valley. In earlier times they were often the victims of Tangkhul raids. Today, however, many of them call themselves Naga, and the Naga federation is glad to add them to their number. The **Kuki** (or Kuki-Chin) are another people who "became" Naga in the 20th century. In the 18th century these people had lived in Manipur, but they caused so much trouble by raiding that many of them were driven down to the Bay of Bengal. In the 20th century a group of them worked their way up to Manipur again. Some members of this later group, known sometimes as Thadou, call themselves Naga.▲

FACTS ABOUT THE NAGA

Population: At least one million.

Location: Nagaland, an Indian state bordering on Burma (Myanmar); within Burma itself; and in the Indian states of Assam, Manipur, and Arunachal Pradesh.

Environment: Steep hillsides separated by wide valleys.

Language: Varying languages in the Tibeto-Burman family.

Main Activities: Farming; trading with other Naga groups and plains people; woodcarving; weaving.

Main crops: Wet rice, dry rice, millet, maize, taro, ginger, chillies, cotton.

Domestic Animals: Fowl, pigs, and mithan (a cross-breed of ox and bison).

Game Animals: Fish, elephant, monkey, deer, wild buffalo.

GLOSSARY

ang The chief of a Konyak village.

bridewealth An exchange of gifts between a groom and his bride's family.

dhou Long multipurpose blade, used for harvesting and carving.

egalitarian Describing a society without a ruling class.

Feast of Merit Naga custom in which a wealthy person holds a feast for the whole village to gain social status and redistribute his wealth.

gaonburas Naga people hired by the British to enforce colonial laws in Naga villages.

hazoa Slanted stone that serves as a ritual center in a Zemi village.

Inner Line Regulation Ruling enacted by the British in 1866 to protect the boundaries of the Naga Hill District.

jhum "Slash-and-burn" agriculture: The trees are chopped down on an area of land, and then the field is cleared of logs and undergrowth by burning.

log gong Long drum made of a single tree trunk, hung outside the *morung* in a Naga village.

morung Large wooden building in the center of a Naga

village, used as a dormitory for young men.

mithan Large, gentle cross-breed of ox and bison, used for sacrifice among most Naga groups.

Naga Hills District Area designated by the British colonial government in 1866. The independent Indian government later placed it under the control of the government of Assam.

Naga National Council (NNC) The leading Naga nationalist group, formed in 1928.

Nagaland A state in the Indian Union, including the area inhabited by about half of the Naga peoples.

Phizo, A. Zapho Naga nationalist leader.

puthi Lhota village priest.

ratsen Shaman in the Lhota villages, specializing in curing the sick.

terhomia In the Angami belief system, earthly spirits who interact with people on a daily basis.

tevo Angami spiritual leader, believed to be a direct descendant of the village founder.

thendu Konyak word designating a hierarchical society.

thenkoh Konyak word designating an egalitarian society.

Tibeto-Burman The language family to which all Naga dialects belong.

Tulani Sangtam festival preparing for the harvest.

FOR FURTHER READING

Borgohain, B.K. and Chaudhury, P.C. Roy. *Folk Tales of Nagaland, Manipur, Tripura, and Mizoram.* New Delhi: Sterling Publications, 1975.

Das, Rajat Kanti. *Manipur Tribal Scene: Studies in Social Change.* New Delhi: Inter-India Publications, 1985.

Elwin, Verrier. *The Nagas in the Nineteenth Century.* London: Oxford University Press, 1969.

Government of Assam. *Tribes of Assam Plains.* Gauhati, India, 1980.

International Work Group for Indigenous Affairs. *The Naga Nation and Its Struggle Against Genocide.* IWGIA Document 56, Copenhagen, Denmark, 1986.

Jacobs, Julian. *The Nagas: Hill Peoples of Northeast India. Society, Culture, and Colonial Encounter.* London: Thames & Hudson, 1990.

Maitra, Kiran Shankar. *Nagaland: Darling of the Northeast.* New Delhi: Mittal Publications, 1991.

Mao, Ashikho Daili. *Nagas: Problems and Politics.* New Delhi: Ashish Publishing House, 1992.

Naga Institute of Culture. *A Brief Historical Account of Nagaland.* Kohima, India, 1970.

INDEX

A
Ahom, 57, 58
ang (*thendu* chief), 18, 20, 21, 23, 29
Angami Naga (Angami), 15, 17, 29, 34, 42, 47, 54
animals, domestic, 15, 18
animism, 29, 54
Ao Naga (Ao), 12, 20, 34-35
Arunachal Pradesh, 12, 51
Assam, 12, 47, 48, 51, 57, 58

B
Boro-Kachari, 58
bridewealth, 23
Burma (Myanmar), 11, 12, 39, 47, 51

C
Christianity, 44, 54
clan, 18, 21, 23

D
dhou (blade), 13, 18

E
earth spirit, 29
exogamy, 21

F
farming, 13-15
Feast of Merit, 24-26
federation, Naga, 12, 48-49
festivals, 32-34
fishing, 16

G
gaonburas (hired deputies), 41
Gawang (Konyak high god), 29
genna (taboo), 32-35

H
hilltop peoples, 7, 12-13
Hinduism, 54, 58
house, Naga, 18
hunting, 15

I
India, 39, 46, 51
initiation, 7, 21
Inner Line Regulation, 40
Islam, 54

J
jhum (slash and burn), 13-15

K
Kepenopfu (female creator spirit), 29
khel (ward) 18, 21, 23, 34
Konyak Naga (Konyak), 12, 18, 21, 23, 37, 42
Kuki-Chin Naga (Kuki-Chin), 59

L
land ownership, 23, 24
language
    Nagamese, 53
    Tibeto-Burman, 11, 53
Lhota Naga (Lhota), 31, 34, 42

M
Manipur, 12, 47, 51, 58-59
Maring Naga (Maring), 58
marriage, 21-23
Mising, 57-58
mithan, 7, 15, 24, 34
morung, 7-9, 20-21, 23, 34, 37, 58

N
Naga Hills District, 40, 47
Nagaland (Indian state), 12, 49, 51
Naga National Council (NNC), 46-47, 48

O
oral history, 21
    myths of, 13, 27-29, 37

P
painting, cloth, 35
Phizo, A. Zapho, 47-48, 49
Phom Naga (Phom), 35
plains people, 52, 54
    trade with, 24
population problems, 52
possession by leopard or tiger, 31
puthi (priest), 31

R
ratsen (shaman), 31
Rengma Naga (Rengma), 35, 37, 42
resources, exploitation of, 51-52
rice, wet, 15

S
sacrifices, 31, 32-34
Sangtam Naga (Sangtam), 12, 42

Sema Naga (Sema), 23, 32-34, 35, 42
Shillong Accord, 50
soul, attacked by spirits, 31
status, social, 24-26
system, egalitarian vs. hierarchic, 17

T
Tangkhul Naga (Tangkhul), 58
tattooing, 35
taxation, 42-44
terhomia (earth spirits), 29, 54
terracing, 11, 15
tevo (ritual leader), 17-18
thendu (hierarchic), 18, 29
thenkoh (egalitarian), 17-18, 23, 26, 29
trade, 23-24, 57
tribes, British-invented, 42-44
Tulani festival, 32-34

U
unity, growth of, 41, 44, 54

V
villages, Naga, 11, 17-18

W
War of Naga Independence, 41
warriors, 7, 21
weaving, 35, 57
woodcarving, 34-35
work, 23-24

Z
Zemi Naga (Zemi), 34-37, 43

Photo Credits: ©Anako Editions/Patrick Bernard, V. Sanyu, A. Wodey

Layout and Design: Kim Sonsky